More Watery Still

More Watery Still

Poems

Patricia Young

Anansi

First published in 1993 by
House of Anansi Press Limited
1800 Steeles Avenue West
Concord, Ontario
L4K 2P3
(416) 445-3333

Canadian Cataloguing in Publication Data

Young, Patricia, 1954-
    More watery still

Poems.
ISBN 0-88784-541-X

I. Title.

PS8597.0673M67 1993   C811'.54   C93-093585-3
PR9199.3.Y685M67 1993

Editing: Anne Szumigalski
Cover Design: Brant Cowie/ArtPlus Limited
Cover Photograph: Lee Goreas
Author Photograph: Tony Bounsall

Printed and bound in Canada

House of Anansi Press gratefully acknowledges the support of the Canada Council, the Ontario Ministry of Culture, Tourism, and Recreation, Ontario Arts Council and Ontario Publishing Centre in the development of writing and publishing in Canada.

For Terence

Contents

During Floodseason

ACKNOWLEDGEMENTS

My special thanks to friends who helped me with these poems: Lesley-Anne Bourne, Don Coles, Michael Kenyon, Janice Kulyk Keefer, Margo Louis, Jay Ruzesky, and Terence Young.

My thanks also to the Canada Council, B.C. Culture, the Banff School of Fine Arts, and the editors of the following publications in which some of these poems first appeared: *Canadian Literature, Event, Fiddlehead, Grain, Malahat Review, Prism,* and *Quarry.*

And finally, I would like to thank Anne Szumigalski for her careful reading of the completed manuscript and her exacting editorial suggestions.

Man on the Dust Jacket

When the Body Speaks to the Heart It Says

I am a hunter-gatherer, busy
climbing the high ridge
to watch where birds
will settle. I am flailing
my arms, picking huckleberries
all day long. I don't ask for much —
sex, a piece of cooked meat.
Waist-deep I stop in salal, I am trying to be
ruffed as a grouse. On my knees
at the edge of the lake
I must fathom
how to pull fish from water. I am
animal, you can't blame me, this
is how I was made — hormones
and glands and ancient
predilections. See,
where I sleep by the fire —
my skull so vulnerable, my skin,
no protection at all.
The way I moan
and curl in on myself
I look like a newborn rat.
You may want love, beauty, the ineffable
things but I am not interested
in what you want.

Tobacco Jar, 1867

This is a tobacco jar though we've always used it for honey.
We marvel over the date etched on the bottom because
where we come from nothing
is old as this.

Enameled figures circle the jar.
Around the lower half a man on horseback pursues
thirteen hounds which pursue a white
deer which pursues the man
on horseback. If
the man swung suddenly round
he could smell the animal's hot breath.

Above this scene of everlasting
pursuit three English gentlemen sit on oak barrels.
This trinity observes the chase from a curved distance.
One smokes a pipe, another drinks from a beer mug,
a third one's head is cradled in his arms.

No women grace this jar but we know
women are half of any story told in heaven
or on earth. We decide the deer is a symbol of Woman.

This morning our spoons dip into honey
and we ask again: what does it mean —
the lust for blood, stench
of panic, and the interminable sitting around
on oak barrels?

We sip our tea sweet, the white deer
leaping out of the dogs' jaws
only to find itself breathing down the hunter's neck.

Is this what the men in breeches
and felt hats ponder as they smoke and drink?
And the one head down on the table —
exhaustion or boredom or grief?

The Man on the Dust Jacket

The man on the dust jacket
wears a white shirt open at the collar,
is blond and looks as though he might once
have been a tennis star, like my husband
might look in twenty years.
He's smiling

but his eyes say — *I've lived long enough now*
to know the nights are easy,
it's the days that are getting
so hard. This evening I read
the book several times through

while my husband wonders aloud — is it possible
for a woman my age to fall in love
with a man on a dust jacket?
And if I said yes,

I would like to step into this stranger's table
of contents, his biographical note
and wide smile? Climb the tree
of his body, lie down
in the leaves?

Tonight, in the solid, dark house I stand
on the landing running a finger down
the book's spine. When do I begin
to see past his face to a room

lit by kerosene lamps? He's bent over
an old kitchen table writing
a poem which begins
in confusion

but ends with a man in a panama hat
opening a gate, a woman
in a yellow dress
walking down to the grass
courts by the river.

Trumpeter Swan

Let's say the walkway was slippery
and the water deep, that I was
buoyant and flexible

but occasionally considered
the salty brink. I had a swan once —
milky glass, an ashtray. When I walked

out of your arms I heard a flock
clap through the mountains,
the mighty applause

of wings. That swan fit
in my hand, its smooth weight,
a cold stone. As a child

I'd search the kitchen drawers
for empty packages of *Matinee.*
Open them flat and draw

on the insides trying to perfect
the elegant swoop, unmistakable
trumpet. Once almost extinct,

these birds now honk
in brazen hundreds.
Down at the gorge they kill

time waiting for Alaska
to lighten up, whistle them
home. If words

can migrate continents, yours
were airborne. Let's say
I sang but stopped, that love

is a coming, a going, say
what you like, anything
that comes to mind,

for the first time I wanted
nothing in return. Oh
I had a swan —

snow-white plumage and nicotine
stains, one black bead
and one eye missing.

The Adulterers

That autumn a student lent me a book
bought from a discount table.
I opened it to *The Adulterers*,
words like an Arizona sun.
I read the poem once then closed
the blinds. In the near-dark

I read it again and again until
my eyes grew accustomed
to the fierce glare of a desert,
until I was inside that shabby motel
room, sitting at the edge
of its sagging bed.
I pushed back

the betrayal waiting outside
the poem, the lies repeating themselves
somewhere in the suburbs
or margins. Nothing mattered
except those four walls —
how blind and forgiving
in the midday heat.
Someone knocked

on my office door; startled,
I played dead. In the courtyard —
talk and laughter, students gathered round
the fountain, textbooks open
on their laps. It was

a short poem though long enough
to say the adulterers
took turns
dancing, naked,
in a Shiva mask —

gold lips, skin white as a geisha's—
their faces in the dim room
larger and more beautiful
than life.

I would quote a line
so you might understand
how an affair sordid as this
could ricochet off the heart but I have only
a faint memory of jagged light,
red clay, canyon walls.
I returned the book

to its owner months ago though my fingers
still burn from touching the page
on which a mask drops
to the floor and a faceless
man and woman finally
sleep in each other's arms.
How long did I swivel

in my chair not answering the phone?
When did I notice I was shaking
like someone who's passed
through her own death?
I parted the blinds. Why
Shiva, I wondered, not daring to think
of you or an answer.

The Basics

We're at sea-level, of course,
and the women smell of papaya and crushed
lilac. This morning in the lingerie
department was like wafting
through a garden — all those women
fingering cotton lilies, straps of peach
silk. And their perfumes, musk,
all the creams they spend
on their skin! In other places it is
otherwise. I'm thinking of the boats
full of refugees, stuck between
hopelessness and the stink
of no welcome. After a week
without food they trample each other
for a piece of black bread. In the lingerie
department I yearned heavenward,
became mild blue scent.
Down here the news gets worse
and worse; driven back
into our bodies we all return
savage, stampede to the death.
Each night I knock on your back
asking what is it you know.
If I'm awash it's because nothing
ever changes. Once we crawled
from the sea or was it
the rot of some river bottom?
We were vile and innocent
and hungry then too.

Licorice Root

I don't understand the birdwatcher's
fascination with names and flight

patterns, the details of mating.
But the watching, binoculars
or not, I understand that.

In the garden today
everything falls away in my hands.
Shot to seed — nasturtiums and garlic,
sweet peas let go with a sigh.
Always I am cross-eyed
with this love of ours.
How sometimes it flops down,
a sick dog at our feet.

Yesterday we walked around the lake and already
the licorice is long ago
and far away. Today
in the garden a sunflower leans
against the house, last pillar of a weary
civilization, how it begs
to topple. I reach to yank,
throw it on the compost when I notice
three wrens.

So, it's they who've scattered empty seeds
along the path. I drop my gloves
and let it stand.

Yesterday in the forest you ran ahead,
rummaged mossy bark and plucked
that root. Grinned
like a boy who's just pulled
a thousand butterflies out of his sleeve.
Later, after warmed-up enchiladas,
the children in bed, you surprised me
again with how much love
is enough. A thousand cocoons
breaking

at once, the taste and the after-
taste — air becoming
a skirmish of wings.

Somewhere His Shoes

My bestfriend has gone, he has gone into
the marble galleries where nothing

ever changes. After he left, the fog
lifted and the house was a shell

hollowed out of sound. Somewhere his shoes
fall mute as the words of politicians

when they speak of honour. He took
an electric razor, his raincoat

and sex. Without its peculiar wisdom
nothing fascinates or is holy.

He has gone but his details endure.
Sometimes he is coming toward me

with the glow of someone alive —
jaw line, stomach muscles, his legs

stepping out of the bath. Clocks
are not much use now that he's gone.

I sit at the kitchen table wearing
his sweatshirt, one cuff smudged

with marmalade. Now the streetlights
switch on like a row of full moons.

In the Ravine

Who could sleep?
Nights I woke to the torrent
that once roared through the valley.
In the city's memory forests still flourished
in swamps — huge conifers and seed-ferns.
We dropped into the ravine
and the world was pungent as yeast,
it hummed for thousands of miles.
All week I spun, a compass berserk,
the needle searching for star or good omen.
Pressed my face against a subway
window unable to navigate
the heart's circumference.
In October light declines so we followed it:
just us and the city's smallest
inhabitants. The children
flew along the gorge, bright
pterodactyls. Time had not begun.
Later, we climbed steps pounded into
rock while behind us
thunder lizards
rose from mud the velvet colour
of apricots. I headed south
into rush hour traffic
and you drove north to your wife and sons.

Among the Yellow Lilies

I was in the garden pulling morning
glory off the fence when she
dropped between my legs.
I hadn't felt a pang,
not a flicker of pain.
Like a pearl she must have
formed in secret. All morning
I'd been yanking but when I reached
behind the peony she slid
from my body; among the yellow lilies —
an easter egg, the only one
my children hadn't found.
I took off my gloves and held her
in one hand, she was
that small. Unlike my others
this one was serene, translucent.
She had that fetal face
we recognize as alien or divine.
I lingered that day
and all week
believing she would waken,
in time, she'd cry out.
The seasons came and went.
Though the storms of January
slammed the coast I stood beside
the fence holding to her

with a love that darkened
the world. This spring
trumpet flowers twine
the stone figure I've become
and still her bluish lids
do not open.

Fantastic Revenge

From the amazing clutter
of your bedroom floor I pick up
a piece of paper. At first I think
this drawing's another of your intricately
worked-out dramas — lasers and bombs
and horrible aliens. There's a globe, too,
stick-figures shooting

out its sides; thin lines attach them
to balloon-cries for help. I am
fascinated by these plots of inter-planetary
warfare. I have watched you bend over
your small desk for hours, listened
to the explosions in the back
of your throat as though listening
to any song of love. *Tell me*

about this picture, I say, and when you do
I learn the horrible alien is not
an alien at all but the woman
at the corner store, the one who
shrieks when you track mud
in with your boots, who
glowers and pinches the back of your neck
if you dawdle too long near the candy.

But the stick-figures
flailing into nothingness, who
are they? *Kids*, you explain, *the store lady's
so mean she's kicked all the kids
off earth.* And then you turn
the page over.

On the reverse, the woman's been flung off
the globe, this wicked hoarder
of candy rockets through
space like a BB gun's pellet

while the stick-kids
march round the curled edges of their universe
carrying signs — *at last we are free.*

Your Junk's Filling Up the World
—*for Liam*

It is no exaggeration to say
I adore
every cell
of your body, every
pore of your skin, the sound
of your voice calling
on a night when the wind is a ram
battering your window.
Your hand,
the way it holds
a pencil. The small C-shaped scar
on your cheek left after
chicken pox, the way you slouch
home after school dragging your knapsack.
How you argue through dinner! —
a courtroom lawyer
who leaves no stone unturned
in his defence of what's
fair for kids.
I am helpless
when you ask my opinion of a hockey player's
skill, when I overhear you
advise a friend
on how to deal with
a bully — *run away fast.*
Your laugh is a lime
drink bubbling
inside my head, I am crazy
for your kisses, the way

you dole them out
like Black
Magic
chocolates, oh, I know you
are too old
for this kind
of talk, I see your eyes
groan heavenward but there is
nothing about you
that does not transport me —
your collection of cereal
rings, popsicle
sticks, to you
every bottle cap is precious,
every elastic
band's got value
and though I complain
your junk's filling up the world
it would not be stretching the truth to say I love
every bit of that junk.

Your Making

We lie on my bed discussing your ancestors.
Your mind folds back one generation, and then back
several more until you are looking up
at your great-great-grandfather
on your father's side —

the German wine-taster. This
is my favourite part of the day, listening
to you think aloud, breathing all of you in.
Tonight you realize how many people went into
your making. *Your making*? Exactly how

were you made? And we've been through
all this before, every few years I outline
the bare mechanics of sex and each time you listen

only to forget. But at eight
you want an answer you can carry sure as a torch
into any future. Your horror
doesn't surprise but your sympathy does.
To make me, you had to do that?
As though your father and I

undertook the unbearable
knowing it would be you all along.
You decide not to return to your own bed
but all night you keep your distance.
Darling, I am sorry

for the facts, they caught me unaware.
For the act itself. Its wild
preposterousness: absurd
as cactus between us.

Geese and Girls

At the end of summer you are
thirteen and bored at the cabin, ask
to walk alone the three miles
to Prior Lake. Your body

is restless as though after years
of sleep it wants to step out, look
around. No, I say, thinking of trucks
parked in the woods, beer tins
strewn along the dirt road.

You plead: just as far
as the stream, then, the first bridge.

This afternoon you and your cousins
swam in the lake. From the wharf
your father and I watched. Geese
slid through the water while you floated
on your back, arms and legs
sprawled over an inner
tube and I thought of a bird
grown too big for its nest.
A playpen, you sneer,

I'll be twenty-one and still
living in a playpen. And if I said,
ok, but carry this bread knife,
for protection take this small axe?
I know curiosity,
how it riots

the blood, you want to bang on the door
of the world. But I am every mother
whose child's been gutted,
thrown in some ditch.
Weeping you say

it's my fierce attitude you hate,
O my girl, I
hate it too.

A Treeless Country

Our family is as wide as the tundra and our habits
roam a treeless country.

No darkness dark enough for our eyes.

We gather round a table of ice and our mother
points to stars forming above the bay.
When we are sad she recites tales
of a time when summer
plains bloomed small horses.

We are a marvel of adaptation — our white fur
in a land of snow. On top of the world
we huddle, thick-coated
and layered in fat.
On frozen slabs we float

into thaw and when we wake
the earth's tipped
toward the sun. In seven days
there will be more light.
Soon: the weary circling
of flies beneath a whitewashed
heaven but for now we can only imagine

the sea's abundant shelves.
Our mother washes us down
with her astonishing
tongue, she speaks
slowly so we understand the cold
truth of our lives.

Words like *huge* and *paw*
swing a deadly blow. *Fish*, she says, *seal.*
These and other edible things.

The Gift
— for Penny

We were all there, eating a meal at the round
oak table. I'd never seen so many
seated together in the summer
kitchen. Former lovers and those
we might love in the future
had all been invited. And children
of every possible union.
Then footsteps on the porch.
No one rose

to answer the knock, everyone too busy
discovering how they'd come to be there —
in New Hampshire in spring, and then
the knock again, louder
on the heavy wooden door.
A man in apron and baker's hat
entered with a brown paper
bag but the bag

was not filled with loaves of warm
bread, it was full of pyjamas, a new pair
for each child. Without argument
the children disappeared to undress
and when they returned we called
their pet names —
sweet lamb, dynakins, missus bean.
In bare feet they wandered the farmhouse

glowing and now that I think of it —
the children were all the same
size, same age, they wore
the same drowsed expression —
each one in baggy trousers and blue

quilted jacket. We turned back to the cold
food on our plates because it hurt
to look at them. The children belonged
to that night in New Hampshire
in a way they would never
belong again and it hurt to watch them
drift into separate
corners of sleep.

Naked Women

Pregnancy

It happens like this: you are a child
yourself, not sure of the details,
you were drinking
milk with that boy in his mother's
kitchen, eating cold lasagne, earlier

you'd walked on the beach. Just
once, just like that, a slip
of the tongue? A visit
to the doctor's and you wait
by the phone. Her voice travels

from Jupiter, hesitates — *positive.*
You tumble backwards, the solar system
blacks out. You pretend
as children do: it isn't so.
Become inventive as the wind, dress

in smocks and breeze past your friends.
They don't notice as you fill
more and more space. Alone
in your bedroom you unbutton
your blouse, suck in your breath,

you stand before the mirror, see,
you are slim as a reed.
And then the butterfly
wings, the kick below the ribcage.
In the bath your stomach shifts

like a land mass. You hate it hate it, rock
all night, not sure who it is
you are wailing for.
In time your body forgets
you, begins to speak

another language. In the middle
of a sentence it walks away
from the boy in your French class,
his white sportscar already a loose
speck in the distance.

Beginning of a Terrible Career

I lit matches, one igniting the other
behind the bathroom's locked
door. I liked slugs

too. After dark in the garden
with an empty ice-cream bucket and red
flashlight. Cabbage and lettuce and
the leaves of roses.
I stood over

the pedestalled sink and watched the flame
burn down to my fingers.

I worried it was the beginning of a terrible career.

With gloved fingers I curled back
the green and harvested
voracious pearls.

Always I opened the window to release the smoke-smell.
Though sometimes my mother screamed: *have you
been burning matches again you're going
to be the death of us yet how many
times have I told you.*

In the middle of the baseball diamond I turned
the slugs onto the grass as though turning
bread dough onto a kneading board.
I set fire

to the matchbox last.
Flushed the charred bits down the toilet
and rinsed the sink. On the ground, the clump

of slugs looked like an exposed brain.
Beneath the moon, an unintelligible mass
disentangling itself. Families

are like that, they don't notice what you're doing
unless they think you're going to burn
the house down.

Hand-Me-Downs

After dinner my mother sorts through
the box of hand-me-downs
my aunt dropped off this morning —
what's threadbare, what's got some life
in it yet. I like the striped
coveralls, the Minnie Mouse t-shirt,
there's an orange cardigan with
jack-o-lantern buttons.
Near the bottom —

a pair of white sandals and I buckle them on.
My mother pushes her fist
into sock after sock, tosses them onto
the discard pile but the green
leotards she keeps for cold
mornings in winter, and then I discover

the dress — my cousin's sundress with the full
yellow skirt. My mother pulls it
over my head, ties the belt
then pivots me round.
Her eyes burst

into flame and I run
from the room where she kneels
on the floor, I run through the house calling
my father. The porch door snaps
shut behind me and he turns

from the chopping block. I twirl
in the dirt. *Beautiful,*
he says, and I want this — my father
leaning on his axe, froe in one hand,
cedar shake in the other, even
the dizziness, I want the sundress and hot,
summer wind. I am afraid to stop
spinning, of what
he will do if I tell him —
she's alone
in the house and she is burning, burning.

Orphanage

I lay on the bottom bunk, my sister
floating above me in the dark
saying she was not my *real*
sister but a changeling
born of the royal family
and dropped at birth on our doorstep.

That was the summer we lived in a run-down
duplex on Partridge Avenue; six oak trees
in the front yard and across the street,
behind a high wire fence — a huge, brick
orphanage. The grounds were vast
and Victorian and wooded beyond

our imagining. Was it
the ordinariness of her life
my sister could not bear — those hot nights
the bedsprings creaked above me,
her saying the king and queen must have
thought it best that their daughter

be raised by common people.
I for one
believed absolutely
that she'd descended from
greatness and for several weeks
acquiesced to her demand, addressing her always

as *your royal highness.*
That was the summer we stood
on our side of freedom
looking through a chain-link fence
hoping to see for ourselves —
a real, live orphan. Once, a few kids

spotted us lurking like poachers
at the edge of their homeless
estate and stayed to talk all afternoon.
Later in bed, my sister and I invented
their harrowing childhoods —
what really went on

behind those walls of ivy.
There was the boy named Bobby.
His father logged up north
though his mother
watched over him every day
from heaven, oh, his mother lived in heaven

and when she walked down the sidewalk
there were angels everywhere!
In fuzzy pyjamas, you know,
the kind babies wear with those soft,
padded feet. And my sister,
flicking a ladybug

off her knee, told how
her real parents were going to drive up
in a coach any day soon
and carry her away
to Windsor castle where she'd sleep
in a pink canopy bed. I can still hear

Bobby's world-weary voice
describing the spare
room his mother'd prepared for him —
floor to ceiling shelves
for the model airplanes he was going
to build from kits. Mostly

I remember him bragging
that she never stepped out
of her bungalow in heaven
without leaving
a note
and all the doors open.

Miss Harkins

Her favourite hymn's on page 144 —
My Heart is Steadfast, O
God. She has no children

and says my eyes are the colour
of appleseeds. She builds my sisters
and me a red table with four

small chairs. She carves the backs
of the chairs into rabbit
shapes. We sit down to miniature

blue willow and bunny ears spring
from our shoulders, they jut
like wings on either

side of our heads. She invites me
to her house for dinner.
There's a piano but no

husband. She wears a yellow
pantsuit and serves food
I've never tasted. I like eating

in the dining room, the spaghetti
more than the meatballs.
After dinner I pound

the keys with tomato
sauce fingers. I don't want to go
home, I ask to come

back. Sundays I stand beside her
at church and she doesn't
give me the look, the one that says —

for chrissakes can't you
sing softer? She says
my eyes are the colour

of appleseeds, *O God*
is my soul waiting in silence.
I sing as loud as I can.

Cousin

In a straw hat I followed A.
through the woods behind her mother's house.
Already it was hot. At the green
edge of morning I dangled
my feet while she entered the pond —
a knife entering its own reflection.

Three years older and when she played
the violin in her room at the top
of the house the notes vibrated,
stuck like wet stars to my skin.

I walked behind A.
through fields and gardens,
her feet treading windfallen apples, straw.

Even now I cannot explain
why tumblers and glass bells exploded
at my touch, clocks stopped
when I placed my hand upon them,
why the strings of her instrument
snapped when I moved too near.

Those crushed nights of August we'd strip
to our underclothes. For hours —
her bow asking and my heart
with its unwavering answer.

My cousin's passion was for hunting out wild
pears, moss — anything
that would scrunch underfoot
but mine was for the swamp-girl
rising out of black water, for the shocking
dark sight of her — clumps of vegetation
clinging to stomach and thighs.

All these years later what should I name it —
infatuation, awe?

Sweet idiocy of girlhood! how I loved
the earth yielding beneath her —
those last days of summer
when I walked behind A.,
she of the peculiar,
dipping gait.

Skipping Song

When I return it is late afternoon
and my sister is skipping on the street.
Her best friends sing and turn the wooden ends —
on the mountain stands a lady,
who she is I do not know.
A black cat

stretches out on the rock wall
soaking up granite
heat. I know
those paws, paws so white.
All week my sister shouted *scram.*

I hardly recognize her
without her glasses, and is that me
beneath the dogwood, kitchen
scissors shoved inside my cardigan?
All week I've stood on the porch,

thrown myself into a hill of sand.
Fallen
and fallen
into the arms of no one.
Now my father is in the driveway stirring
cement. Every kid knows —

one cut and the whole tree dies.
I snip off a twig because
it's forbidden, because it's against
the law, because it will serve them all right
if I go
to jail. I stick the yellow flower
into my buttonhole and wait
for the sirens to begin
screaming toward me.
I hear nothing

but sand

slipping from shovel
to wheelbarrow, the soft whip
of rope as it hits pavement —

all she wants is gold and silver,
all she wants is a fine young man.

I've returned because the cat
now draped like beads around my neck
will soon slide from my body.
Because I must go to the man in the faded
blue skullcap, I must
pull his head down,
tell him

I will never love anyone more than
I love him at this moment. I've returned
because how else could I know

the dogwood survives
my single act of butchery.

Merry-Go-Round

I'd be waiting on the front porch
for Danny Bowles to ride up
on his bike ringing
his bell. Every afternoon
at 4:00 he delivered the *Times*

and every afternoon I'd spread the newspaper
on the dining room table, turn
straight to the comics. A ritual
that completed my world and nothing since
has compared to that dogged

repetition. One spring
my father built
a merry-go-round
out of scraps of wood and a metal
bedstead. From my gabled attic

window the backyard was an orchard,
the merry-go-round — a pinwheel
spinning deep within
its foliage. The sky
was big then too and some nights

stars hung in branches low as pears.
For years I slept inside a house
of many doors, a vegetable
dreaming dark, tuberous dreams.
Beyond the open windows:

lawnmowers, airplanes, dragonflies,
every winged and buzzing thing
beating its way in. When I woke
I turned to the comic page
but *Nancy* wasn't funny,

Sluggo had always been a bore
and later that night Danny Bowles
turned his bike back in my direction.
I must have stolen
down the fire-escape because suddenly

there he was — tall as a torch — and I
promised myself always to know love
that way, as something bright and burning.
The merry-go-round glinted in moonlight.
While my parents slept

we jumped aboard, pumped fast,
then faster. How we mocked
the slowly turning
earth, that night our urgency
startled even us.

First Love

He turns off the light and drags a kitchen chair
into the centre of the room. He sits, pulls me onto
his lap. I wrap my arms and legs around
all of him, hold his head close.
We stay that way a long time,
saying nothing.

In a week he will fly to England. It's the end
of August and for two hot days we shop
for things he will need to backpack through Europe.
He buys me a James Taylor record,
it's the first record I own.

The night before he leaves we go to a party.
I stand on the back porch. A huge willow tree
canopies the yard. From inside the house
I hear him say, *where's she gone?*
Green light slides down the branches.

In September I return to school.
My friends treat me with a new kindness, I have
the status of a woman whose husband has gone to war.
For three months I write letters every night
after dinner, I sit cross-legged
on my bed listening to *Sweet Baby James.*

At the end of November I bundle the letters
in a box and bring them to his mother.
She will deliver them in two days
when she meets him in Italy.
At the Rome airport, wouldn't you know it,
she loses that one suitcase.

He flies home for Christmas.
I walk into his bedroom and he's got his arms
around a woman who's weeping,
stroking his cheek.
For a moment I can't decide
and then I recognize his mother's voice.

I can't move —
the sight of them embracing like lovers.
His mother looks over his shoulder, she stares
through me as though I'm a glass girl.

I sit in the kitchen and wait for him to remember
last summer. His youngest sister
comes in and opens the fridge door, she is
looking for ice-cream. The lightbulb's
broken and the room remains dark.

Then she is a blind animal moving toward the sound
of a heartbeat. Blond and marsupial,
she climbs the front of my body.
She sits on my lap and begins
to play with my hair.

Popovich Resthome
— *for Dianne*

At seventeen Philip Keller thought a plastic bag
of marijuana a romantic gift. *Thanks,*
we'd say and smoke it at the beach after work.
Those days we hitchhiked everywhere,
high-grade Colombian spilling
from our fingers and
the pockets of our jeans.

Saturday mornings we raced through Beacon Hill,
late, half-dressed. At the resthome
slopped eggs and toast onto breakfast trays,
stewed prunes for everyone whether
they liked them or not. Beyond
the clouded eyes of old folks
strapped into chairs

I loved you
as much as Philip, and remember
Mr. Sharkey, a conductor all his life:
*girls, girls, how long till the train
arrives in Winnipeg?*
Mrs. Darby, a shrivelled seed
of a woman, though when we tried
to spoon-feed her she clawed
our faces like a drowning
cat. Or Mr. O'Connor,

Irish and threatening always
to return to the run-down hotel
he'd lived in for years. He'd bang
his cane against the commode till we stopped
washing dishes to pat *Old Spice*
on his cheeks. Mrs. Popovich was also

a seamstress, all day bent over the Singer.
In the backroom sewed wedding gowns,
oblivious of the shit and vomit and drugged
moaning. But the world also smelled
of gardenias, it was
spring and Philip Keller

was in love
with you, then me, then
you, a weather-
cock, and we never knew
which way the wind would turn his head.
And the night he met us after work.
Whose idea that we slip

from the grime of our skins
and those gravy-stained shifts into long
white dresses? We grabbed Philip
and flew into the street,
down an avenue of blossoming trees,
waving at Mrs. McGavern where
she rocked and hallucinated
at an upstairs window.

Two brides, she insisted
the next morning. *As God is my judge,*
two brides and one groom!

Boyfriends

I stumble over baskets of unfolded laundry
to answer the phone and it's my best
friend from high school playing

Carmina Burana loud
in her living room, listen,
she says, holding the mouthpiece up

like a microphone and then she's asking,
do you remember that spring, our
boyfriends joining

the university choir? That was
the year my parents divorced and I moved
into my sister's apartment,

those sunlit rooms on the top
of that old house, current bushes
dripping clumps of magenta

in every corner of the yard, and
the night they sang at the Royal Theatre,
god they were handsome in rented

tuxedoes and white running shoes,
later walking home, the streets
canopied with cherry blossoms, we

might have been catapulted out
of the 13th century, passing round
a bottle of cheap Kelowna wine,

our boyfriends singing, *come my darling,*
come with joy, or bursting into
the chorus of *O Fortuna*

and love, love flew everywhere, and
mine was a tenor and yours
was a second bass.

Naked Women

On the phone my sister says,

did I ever tell you about that magazine
of naked women? The one Hilary found under
the driver's seat of her father's Pontiac?

Hilary's dad! Ludicrous
to imagine him driving to the shipyard at 7 a.m.,
lunchbucket rubbing his thigh. Stopped
at a red light and flipping through the pages.

They stood before full-length mirrors,
my sister says, *I guess for a front*
and back view.

I ask if the women wore anything, on their feet,
for instance, did they wear those fluffy
pink slippers, can she remember
high-heel sandals? And their hair—
was it back-combed, done in French rolls?

For godsake, she says, *it was a long time ago,*

though I remember like a blast from yesterday
that Pontiac's horn, jumping up and down
in the back seat, Hilary's father
driving us to the peninsula where we stole
vegetables right from the fields.
On the way home crunching small dirty carrots.

Actually they were quite tasteful,
my sister says, *today those photographs*
might be considered art.

After we hang up I can't let go
of those women, of wanting them to mean
something else. Who knows? Maybe
they'd been working in the garden all afternoon.

I want the phone to stop ringing,
the baby to cease crying, dirt under the fingernails.
I want those women to be somebody's mother
after she's peeled off her blouse
and shorts and turned unthinking
toward the mirror.

Our own mother perhaps. On each page
her look of exhaustion before
stepping into the bath.

The Pie Story

Soon after they married, our father asked
our mother for an apple pie. And so
she measured flour and lard,
flicked ice-water by the handful
but the stuff wouldn't stick, and still
it wouldn't stick and finally she shouted,
do it yourself, goddamnit, it won't stick!

Who were those people who shaped our lives
as though they were lumps of obstinate
dough? Without this photograph
we could not summon their young faces —
the woman in a wedding suit, her smile,
a slash of black lipstick.
The man taller than we remember,
and sometimes there doesn't seem any point
trying to see back over mountains
of cores and spiralled yellow peels.

Years later it did stick
and our mother'd spend whole days
in the grip of a rolling pin, shoving aluminum
plates into the oven. The smell of baking
apples, hot sugar, us squabbling over
the extra bits of pastry that fell
from her paring knife as she told
the pie story —

how our father dropped to his knees—
you've never seen anything so ridiculous,
a grown man, almost in tears!

We'd stop then. Stop pressing scraps
into grubby little tart shells to imagine him
kneeling on the red linoleum of that first
kitchen — *just once more, please try again.*

Oldest to youngest we'd step into
the space between our father's
plea and the white dust of our mother's
cheek. Stand in the clarity of that moment —
day's last light spilling into the empty
tin canister.

Choosing a Picture to Live With

You can find my mother in the graveyard.
It is not death she is drawn to but
the unruffled sky, the place
itself, so sure of its purpose.
We are kind to the dead,

give them a sea-side residence,
a superb view. She walks the labyrinth
of paths scattering long-stemmed
carnations. Among chestnut

trees and marble tombstones
she is a tartan sail, her skirt flapping.
Growing up I rarely saw
my mother outside the dowdy
clothes of household chores.
Once I writhed

in my desk at school — Visitors' Day
and where was she? I think
I gasped aloud. A flash
of lipstick, black curls —
a movie star who'd wandered into
the wrong set? Washed up
against the world

map, my mother obliterated
pale seas, pastel continents.
These days she's drawn to the cemetery.
Every bitter word tucked away,
nothing left but love
abridged, composed on stone.

Again I twist and crane
my neck, again she stops to read
some tragic dates, moves toward, but
cannot reach, my father's grave.

On earth we have no choice
but to bend to grief, we must choose
a picture we can live with.
If she comes this way
I will tell her: *I choose you*

in a red coat
walking through that classroom door.

Black Forest Cake

I walk through the cemetery
balancing a cakebox on top of my head.
I am remembering the neighbourhood
boy who threw a dirt
bomb at the back of my head
when I was a child who still believed

she could fly. Remembering the thud
against my skull, voices in the kitchen,
my father's anger on the phone.
I am not superstitious; even so,
I step around the graves.
Old chestnut trees

line the paths, they lean away from
the ocean as though cringing from its shout.
Today is my daughter's birthday.
November is also the month
of my father's death.
I remember running

back and forth across the lawn,
flapping my arms — a wind-up toy too tightly wound,
my animal outrage when the rock
shot out of the sky
yanking me down before I'd learned
to lift off the ground.

Today I am shackled
to my earthbound self,
realize it, and not the random
malevolence or sudden mess
of blood, was my first and deepest
disappointment.

At my father's grave I sit
on the marble slab, cakebox beside me.
In the cemetery there's a statue
with blue-tipped wings
and a crushed nose and I try
to be still

as she is
still
while my father cuts
the clumps of matted hair,
washes dirt from the wound with strips
of torn bedsheet.

I lock
eyes with the angel
as my father assures me
a scab will form,
it will harden
and fall away.

During Floodseason

Solitude

I sat at the white desk
under the skylight thinking
of all you'd said. It was raining.
I opened my notebook and wrote a list
of the things I desired most
in the world. I began
with the broad strokes of summer but the list
went on and on. *Solitude*
hung nearby, she was a framed print
of a girl deep in thought.
It was November, that time of year
when we all go searching
for a river, perhaps, where ancient
fig trees grow along the banks.
Solitude's chin pressed into
her palm, she wept
but there were no tears.
A boy marked like a tropical fish
appeared above my head.
On the other side of the skylight
his face slipped through the dark.
Sorrow broke, wave upon wave.
Night was black as leather
and smelled of pumpkins. The boy
with avacado skin swam out of my vision.
I closed my notebook and turned off the lamp.
Things became watery and then
more watery still.

Murals

At Long Beach I sit in a plastic lawn
chair facing the ocean, binoculars
raised. I am looking

for a whale. I would like to tell my children
how its gigantic body leapt
out of the waves
graceful as a minnow.
How it slid, a shimmering blade

back into the foam. I do not know
that sitting at the edge
of the Pacific
I am more likely to see an elephant
tap dance on water.
There is much

I don't know — that the last
whales mutated, their flippers transforming
into wings. That they churned
and flapped their tails
until their thunderous dark
bodies rose into the air.
They flew

toward the cities,
up and down the coast
they swam into the sides of tall buildings:
hospitals, banks, insurance companies.
Spread themselves across
the blank canvases

on every street corner.
A storm whips across the bay.
I have been sitting so long and
I am cold, please someone, tell me
to go home, tell me they are
happy up there

pressed like colossal blue butterflies.
against cement walls.

Radium Hot Springs
— *for Margaret*

There was no point trying to be good.
Two years older you were
good enough for both
of us, and I remember how at five
you walked out
of your body and those awful
middle names — *Agnes McAlpine.*

At the deep end grown-up faces bobbed
like apples so you waded out
toward them — waist,
shoulders, neck, mineral
water swallowed up
your head but when you reached
to pull yourself into
air the railing burned your hand.

You kept walking. Here the story switches
to our mother leaning high above
the pool. On the sideline
her mouth's a frozen
howl, her arms flail in slow
motion, she could be a cheerleader
waving pom-poms at an underwater game.

A man lolling on his back
finally saw and moved with dream-like
sluggishness to intercept
your blurry touchdown.

In the story I tell
you are fished from near-death
already sprouting fins, rosy gills
below the jaw. I say,
my sister's goodness propelled her
to the other side

of drowning, I saw her bathingsuit
breathe purple
scales onto her skin.

During Floodseason My Son Remembers

We're lying beneath the skylight
when he tells me he's no longer mad
I locked him in the car
trunk. Car trunk?
Surely you dreamt this.
He excuses me also

for hauling him by one foot
across his bedroom floor.
A dream too, I insist, but no,
he remembers the pyjamas — red and blue
race cars, lotus and porsche.
He guesses he was three
but still his cheek burns
to remember being dragged
across the rust carpet.
He's so convinced

I can almost recall rage
monstrous as this, gripping
a thin ankle. And there's more —
the time I packed his lunchkit
with nothing but cake.
Even his thermos was empty, just
stale cake. Tonight water spills
from sky and gutters and he tells
how he sat alone at the daycare
table while the other children
ran out to play. In a hot
orange kitchen chewed

and gagged, unable to swallow.
Ah, I say, *dreams are like that,*
they get stuck in your throat.
Against the glass rain batters and
he remembers the duck slippers on his feet,
Amelia's doll beside him in a chair.
Tonight my son leans over
to pat my cheek:

it's ok, he says.
Real or imagined is not the point.
Beyond these walls the world drowns.

Instructions in a Lost Country

You are in lost country and your flashlight
surprises even the mountains.

Something dark is sloping through the underbrush.

Rattle your noisemaker, your tin can of stones.

Tell yourself what you need to believe —
that light in the valley offers escape.

In high country travel into the wind.

Something is trying to identify you.
Watch for signs — a white patch across the throat.

Near rushing water blow your whistle.
A cinnamon muzzle moves among the pines.

In this forest nothing but the infuriating
smell of your fear springs into
existence. Talk. Sing.

Something is snapping its jaws, something
with laid-back ears
rears up on hind legs.

No tree to climb, no flight without wings.

The taste of your blood is trapped in the river bottom.

Love is dangerous in any season.
You knew that when you stepped off the trail.

Where Cows Once Pastured

In the photograph my daughter and I
lean against a porch rail, velvet with moss.

It's New Year's Eve and quiet as the world
before the forest began. We're in running shoes,

t-shirts, we've been jogging down past
the marsh where cows once pastured.

Lately, I've begun to speak in shortcuts,
is it any wonder? The way the mind must leap,

the river traffic always jammed. Looking
at her face, cloudless as a fireweed

day in summer, it's hard to believe
she's ever been sad. In the photograph

we've forgotten the night stumbling punch-
drunk into another year, our cells falling away

like sand. We're doing nothing on the porch
and she's telling me the winds of Burma

blow in from the Indian Ocean, for months
they blow in the same direction.

On the Roof

All afternoon I stalk the roof's incline, lonely
as a chimera. Tiled eaves slope into
the garden and the sky
is a field of blue poppies.

So many girls pass below me
on their way home from school.
Nothing escapes me, up here
I am grotesque,
all eyes.

I look down through the skylights
and long to enter the rooms beneath —
pyjama bottoms crumpled
in a corner, a stray running
shoe balanced on a stair,
Treasure Island open beside a child's bed.
Every detail grafts to my heart.

I grow solid in the shadow of ash
trees, resigned to my goat's
body, serpent's tail. Now
a boy on a mountain
bike rides past waving
one hand, a mother pushes a buggy
along the sidewalk — my lion's head stretches so far
beyond the gutter. Even her baby
looks up and claps.

I open my mouth
to ask *where is my daughter*
but something high
and clear
pours
and pours out.

The Dead Body of My Friend

I was given the dead body of my friend
but I did not dress her in white, I did not
dig a place in the forest or throw
hyacinths into her grave.
I am afraid to think

of what I have done. If you knew
you would not eat beside me on the terrace,
you would not offer me another tangerine.
I should tell someone,

the police or my oldest sister.
Listen: I was given the arms and legs,
the fine head of my friend but I did not
cover them with pine needles.
Once, I came upon

this friend, naked and washing
her dog in the river.
When she led it onto the bank
I saw how old and blind
the dog had become.
From a bridge above
I watched her wind up the path,
encouraging each limping step.
I will go

look for my friend.
I must tell her what I have done and not done.
There she is now guiding the animal
out of the water

Revelation

I walk beneath the blue mountains, nothing
gets in my way. At the duckpond
gulls hunch like small thugs, bully and scrap
for a piece of dry bread. I walk until
I arrive at the sea, because I have
a notion my body will one day lift off
these cliffs. This morning
the cream turrets of *Alcatraz*
light up in a brief ray
of sun, huge breakers crash and melt
into sand, and I remember
rain, boredom so intense I was
terrified I'd jump out of my desk and
never stop screaming. Remember
my fifth grade teacher opening a book,
reading a poem aloud — waves were white
horses — sitting bolt upright because
it was true! — their frothing
bodies, foam tails lashing the air.
Today those same waves buck and hiss
and throw back their heads and I
remember looking past a woman
in a gray, pleated skirt, out and beyond
the smeared windows to where the sky
opened. In that moment tangerine
light flooded the classroom
and it was not a classroom at all but
the holy city of New Jerusalem,
and the former things had passed away.

The Wisians

Wisians are a fictitious group, added by poll takers to
a list of ethnic groups in order to test the respondents
in a study of ethnic images in the United States . . .
Forty percent of those surveyed gave Wisians a relatively
low average rating of 4.2 on a nine-point social scale.

New York Times

And so we came across the turbid waters, sailing
from a country so far back, so deeply
embedded in memory only you
knew its name.

With our ancients and our translucent
children, in ocean-going vessels, alongside
bolts of English cloth.
Inside wooden hulls, from early
April to late November.

Fleeing drought and oppression,
hungry for fresh food and white-
collar jobs. Jammed between sacks
of Pennsylvanian flour, West Indian sugar.
To invent a life for ourselves.

With bird symbols — woodpeckers and crows —
stamped on our foreheads.

We dropped our old skins right where we stood.
We were foreign without sounding like foreigners.
Our vague features were swallowed up fast.

We drifted toward your cities as though
we'd been drifting that way for centuries.

But no one was paying attention.
No one noticed at the docks when we slipped
into the crowds wearing long coats
pounded out of tortoiseshell and bark.
No one complained to the Department of Immigration.
No one broke bread with us or bothered
to turn us back to where
we came from beyond the roiling sea.

Raking the Moon

I was raking the moon out of the water.
It had dropped into the sea.
I raked and raked but could not
draw the moon out. The sea was empty.

I was shovelling light through the front door.
I'd been raking since morning, holy mary
mother of god, what
was the moon —

eggyolk, grapefruit, bright yellow button?

There were no windows in the rooms
of my house. I was tired
of the bruises on my shoulders and hips.
Tired of bumping into hard, clay things.

As soon as day broke the moon dropped
below the equator. First I was
hungry and then I was hungry for passion
fruit. Morning fell
on the doorstep — thick slices of quick light.

It was serious work, shovelling it in.
Something, not a halo, whirred above my head.
Night without a moon, a house without day?
Sweet jesus, I kneeled at the front door.

There was nothing to hang in the sky.
The sky was empty and passed like a bruise
over the tropics. I was raking
with all my strength, I was strong
and shovelling, oh I was tired!

It happened so fast — I was sucked up, drawn into.
It might have been palm leaves slicing
the dark, it might have been blades
of shuddering light.
I entered

the fan's pure steel
hopeful and glad
and serious about love.